PRAISE FOR HEIDI SANDER

"I am deeply touched by this piece. The language is fluid, impactful, and spare and the attention to sensory detail is divine. The voice is genuine and absolutely breaks my heart. I found myself haunted by it, returning again and again to the sanctuary of that sacred kitchen.

Thank you again for bringing this piece into the world. I am grateful for your voice."

— STACY R. NIGLIAZZO,
AWARD-WINNING POET, *SKY THE OAR* AND *SCISSORED MOON*

"In *The Forest of My Mind*, poet Heidi Sander takes the reader on a heartfelt journey of recovery from grief. Her voice threads the labyrinthine forests of the soul in search of a clarity that only great suffering and emergence can bring. The book echoes the organic and marvelous structure of a pine tree, beginning with the roots buried in a profound sense of loss and ending in the redemptive recognition of highest boughs and needles that reach for the light. These poems are memorable and exquisitely crafted."

— BRUCE MEYER,
AWARD-WINNING POET AND AUTHOR,
GRACE OF FALLING STARS AND *TOAST SOLDIERS*

"Your poetry is diverse and roaming; the energy is strong and the feeling is evoked in the imagery and word choices that reveal the many layers and tensions beneath your experience of loss and grief. I also love how you ask many questions, which adds to the voice by giving space for both the reader and speaker to process. Your words not only honor those who have been lost, but quite literally summon them into your body of poems. The collection has a sense of vulnerability that feels universal and easy for readers to trust and embrace. At times you move away from the self/personal/human perspective to expand your scope towards the natural world and what it can reveal about hope, growth, and healing, as well. In terms of form, your acrostic poem is brilliant, which is very hard to achieve with such a level of coherence and meaning. Keep on sharing your work with the world!"

— ALAN CHAZARO,
LAWRENCE FERLINGHETTI FELLOW AND POET OF
PIÑATA THEORY AND *THIS IS NOT A FRANK OCEAN COVER ALBUM*

"Serene and thoughtful…"

— TINY SEED LITERARY JOURNAL

"I think it's very timely for the era that we are living through right now…There is a healing power in poetry and in the arts in general. It soothes our soul in ways that a lot of other mediums can't."

— JESS BRADY,
LET'S TALK LONDON RADIO

"It explores the strength of connection through generations: the persistent hope carried during war and immigration, the traditions that bind pain and beauty, and love that overrides everything."

— BLAIR ADAMS,
KITCHENER TODAY

"I loved how I saw that as well in terms of the renewal part because grief and loss is horribly painful but there is that light at the end of the tunnel."

— PETER MARANGER,
ROGERS

"There were submissions from 19 countries and all 50 states for the award, but Sander's poem stood out for its authenticity and uniqueness."

— SCOTT MILLER,
CTV NEWS

"*How We Live On*, the award-winning poem written by Stratford's Heidi Sander is part of a larger poetry collection she's called *The Forest of My Mind*, comprising poems that feature themes of family, generational history, memory, loss, hope and nature."

— GALEN SIMMONS,
STRATFORD BEACON HERALD

THE FOREST OF MY MIND

Heidi Sander

CROWSNEST BOOKS

The Forest of My Mind

Copyright © 2021 by Heidi Sander

ISBN: 978-0-921332-78-7

All rights reserved.

Book Designer: Jamie Arts

Crowsnest Books www.crowsnestbooks.com

Distributed by the University of Toronto Press

The author greatly appreciates you taking the time to read this work. Please consider leaving a review wherever you bought the book, or telling your friends or blog readers about *The Forest of My Mind* to help spread the word. Thank you for your support.

Printed and bound in Canada

CONTENTS

To the memory of my mom,
you are with me always.

THE WEEK AFTER

Rise and Fall

Your shallow breath
        the only conversation left,
                the only sound I can still hear.
                Remember, I whisper:
                those dolphins following us at the beach,
        climbing the cherry tree with the birds,
singing with crickets at the campfire.

Thank you, for the magic,

        for believing in me,

                I repeat softly,

                with the rhythm

                of your chest,

        a slow rise and fall

of these words.

Uninvited

You are on the hunt, lurking
beneath the shadows,
stealing sleep, snatching
peace, slicing time.

While you slither into her blood,
I hold on with my hands
whispering words, humming,
    helpless
as you seize her cold skin,
occupy her rippled breathing.

I knew you were coming but
I won't name you. You were never
invited,
    yet
you crept closer.

Is it me you want?

Her body has surrendered,
her soul has lifted, far away
from your darkness.

       There is no room for you here.
       She has left her love to fill me.
       It is too rich for your hunger, too deep
       for your greedy fangs.

Flow Like A River

Your hand was locked
around mine, until your
last breath.

The rest of you,
flowed like a river
away from the banks of life,
into the arms of those you loved.

It was up to me
to raise my fingers
and let you go.

Gathering Emptiness

The morning after,
I went out early.
I didn't want to talk,
look into sympathetic eyes,
no condolences, no stories,
no memories, no advice.

No. I wanted to feel each tear
pressing on my heart. To gather
emptiness from dark clouds
covering the sky. I wanted
to be lost where I once
knew the way.

I couldn't cry. Not even
think. Of anything. Not
loss. Not love. Not loneliness.
I walked through
numb streets, over
brittle grass, not
stopping, not looking.

Until the treetops
glowed with light,
and I closed my
eyes and waited
till the earth emerged
from grey shadows.

All morning long, I
walked into the sun,
my heart burning for you.

Snapshot

I cry into the pillow,
in the shower,
with music on.

I wail
when you are not around

sink deeper.

I like it here.

Droplets

In the middle of a cold
      evening, the wind curled
            its angry lip and pummelled

the earth
      with sharp crystals,
            bared his teeth

and tossed
      curtains of ice
            onto strong oak limbs,

pooling them against the
      trunk hollow, weighing
            down each twig and dry

leaf that bobbed
      and twisted in his
            thrashing tail.

Each bough
      rose and fell,
            until all the

bruised branches
      were coated and
            one by one,

creaked, slowly
      drooping onto the
            frozen lap of the earth.

In the morning the sky
          gently glowed, then burned.
                    When the raging gale

retreated, rays of
          light warmed
                    the glazed bark

till the trees glimmered,
          skin softening into blue
                    droplets, arms dripping

and slowly rising
          from the ground,
                    returning to

their place
          in the sky, facing
                    upward and hopeful.

Can you do
          the same with
                    my tears dear heart,

release this raw
          sorrow, lift it up
                    to the luminous sun?

Liquid Air

I hear their yearning cry
while huddled under
the vast sky,
a roof over
my aching heart
that wants to lift
its wings
soar with the geese
through liquid air.

They angle their long necks
toward constellations,
beckoning the arc of the sun,
tilt of the earth's axis,
ancient memories of home.

Where is home now that you are gone?

Silence falls and
the grey clouds open
their windows of rain
into the pool
of my cupped hands.

They will return next spring,
but still,
I cry with the earth,
we both know the sorrow

of being left behind.

Asking Too Much

Roses flicker like bright flames,
the wind rocking their sweet fragrance
on its gentle swing.

Am I asking too much?

Perhaps,
but there are losses I can't yet bear:

the shudder of a bird snatched by a hawk,
the arthritic finger that can't write,

your kneeling here, tending the rose bush.

Dew

Morning light
doesn't breathe yet,
its dark eyes
still closed
and wet with dew.

Do you remember
wading in mudflats
while the Atlantic rose
we stepped into
freedom, strength —

digging clams that morning
cooking over an open flame
cradling the shore
the centre of our being — discovery
we gave each other that —

life's marrow,
a palace of memories,
sun stroking my forehead,
my closed eyes,
weeping.

DEEP LOSS

Visitors

They came when they could, added their initials
to the lines in a binder, the faint edges of
care, didn't see the unwritten pages
of your worries, the hours of questioning
to arrive at difficult answers, holding
your hand till you fell asleep, the fresh berries
of comfort, the sudden midnight calls,
the mad dash to the pharmacy, wrapping
you in blanket layers to stay warm,
reviewing medical plans repeatedly till
there was trust in the system, feeding you
when your arms couldn't lift anymore,
curled up watching the same movie on
repeat till you forgot the clang
of the oxygen tank, my handwritten name
and cell number by the bedside.

You won't find my initials in the binder.

Be Still

1.
There is only silence
as I walk through
this curtain of snow,
enclosing my footsteps,
till I am a ghost
in a white shroud
of stillness.

2.
You let death enter you slowly.
No fear, no shudder, no gasp.
You accepted it, breathed it in.

3.
Stillness was how you did everything,
singing me to sleep,
patching broken skin,
sewing till midnight.

Your life was a flurry of activity,
a house full of children,
demands and obligations,
yet all I ever felt from you
was calm.

4.
And always, unconditional love.

5.
Set aside this poem for a bit,
put away your phone,
and breathe in the essence
of this very moment,

let it linger,
like death will someday,
then,
tell me what you feel.

6.
Meanwhile snowflakes continue
softening the shoulders of trees,
and one ray of light
swims onto the
frozen pathway,
walks onto this page.

These things in life are certain:
the stillness of winter
the stillness of you gone.

On Hold

When they tell you time will heal,
don't believe them. Not in the first
year anyhow,
or even afterwards.
Besides
hasn't everything been said,
written,
sung,
whispered
in the night?

I won't tell you to get on
with your life.
Stay here for now,
tucked away
in a cabin of trees,
where the clock turns
by a different hour.

Grow your roots of sorrow,
sink deep, splash through
darkening clouds, scream at the
stars, replant your heart.

    There's no straight path
    to find your way home.

Unsorted

Every so often,
I find a note,
a doodle,
a cut of fabric,
tucked between
the pages of a book.

It's as if
you're still here.

Sketches imprinted with memories,
lists filled with ideas and plans.
Dreams should never die, right?

Your words swim into
the pooled corners of my heart,
threading the past, stitching
the carved lines
of this moment,
          when I miss you,
                    and find you all at once.

What will we leave behind
once we've departed?

When I am gone,
I want my love to keep giving,
my words to keep living.

The Rhythm of Life

Not long after
the sky's roof shook

with thunder and
split a tree trunk,

a curved nest,
lined with thistle silk

dropped onto another limb.
The hooked finger of night .

gulped it whole.
When the sun stretched

its tired fingers through
the branches, each blue

egg was crushed —
but one.

I know of broken things,
lost dreams,

shattered hopes,
flowers by gravestones

     but if we lift
     the rug of darkness

     behind those thick clouds,
     the sun's marrow turns to starlight

       — a lamp is always on —

Calling you

Years ago,
I called toward
a dark palace of trees,
moments later
silent wings rippled
through the night.

Our hearts bowed
we both pointed,
hands touching mid-air.

For three evenings, I raised
my hands to my mouth,
the owl returned the call.

It was miraculous, you said,
a sign, a nexus.

What is possible with this life
we have?

Tonight I stand among those pines,

Calling you.

Become the Moon

Become the moon

Glow

In your darkest night.

SEARCHING
FOR COMFORT

Fill This Room

Today, along the roadside,
flowers bent their faces
to the light, one broken branch
of an old lilac, dangled
its thick clusters of blossoms,
in the tall grasses.

I couldn't abandon them,
trembling in the morning breeze,
growing all this time
to send their smooth
fragrance into the world.

I gathered the lavender spikes in my arms,
let their limp stalks drink
in a deep pool of water
and set them next to your photo.

> This room wouldn't be empty
> if I could fill it with each
> thought I have of you.

Each day there would be
a new field of flowers, where
butterflies coast into the mouth
of your garden, and the sun
stretches its mane of honey
over the entire pathway.

If I could gather your lifetime of smiles,
the love you gave strangers,
I could build a road infinitely long,
that I could reach you.

I would do it all,
I would do anything,
to see you again.

Rooted
For Oma

When they plowed over the
garden, that's when you truly
died.

What seemed work to others
was your lifeblood.
While everything around you
and within you grew
tired and frail, your
garden seeded the darkness.

Oh you still lived
for years, tending to this
and that, but the garden
was your purpose. You
lived by the rhythm
of it. The first buds
on the peppers, bright bursts of
tomatoes, thick tufts
of lettuce weighted under snow.

You drew strength
from your plants as much
as you gave them life.

When they flattened
the raspberry bushes,
the ones you tended
for decades, you lost
everything all over
again: your home during
the war, your son on the
battlefield.

You sank deeper and
deeper into your recesses,
memory, roots
to hold on to.

Your Tulip

I know loss,
    the shaky doubled-knees,
        raw fists against the wall,
            sobbing into a soft pillow.

I know fear,
    trembling fingers on the face,
        closed wet eyes,
            long piercing screams.

But I also know of hope,
    that moment of sacred happiness
        when the soft petals of your tulip
            open every spring.

Daughter Of The Moon

Looking into the pink
throat of the night,
I become daughter of the moon,
hunter of the stars.

I wish I could bottle this moment,
lap up the fire in my heart,
pour it into the stars for you,

— Wishing —
— Dreaming —

Lighting the way with this poem.

Don't

Don't
Forget
You Loved Deeply

Don't
Change
Who You Are

Don't
Regret
What You Missed

Don't
Worry
About What They Said

Don't
Fear
What You Lost

Don't

Forget

You Are Enough

Evermore
Song for Mom

I held your hand
it was my own,
with me always
till I was grown.

and then you aged
and needed me,
I took your hand
to set you free

I love you always
and evermore
Your heart is in mine
wherever I go
And I know you
are always there
with me.

For many years
we walked together
sharing joys and dreams
entwined forever

then our life journey
was torn apart
now you're in my soul
deep in my heart

I love you always
and evermore
Your heart is in mine
wherever I go
And I know you
are always there
with me.

RENEWAL

Snow and Sky

The sun tightens
a flush kerchief
around snow and sky,
an inseparable bond.

I wake to the thought of you.
I sleep under your peaceful watch
trusting the throat of this storm
won't crash down as death once did,
burying me with questions
the 'why' and 'what for'

Is it faith?

Knowing the clouds
lap up the sleet,
the earth eventually,
absorbs liquid tears
from white pain.

If I could stop the questions,
I would have noticed the ice
dripping from the pink clouds.

How We Live On

1.
The wind empties its pockets of seeds
while I fill mine with apples,
leaving the rest for the deer
whose sleeping bodies etched
the flattened grass.

I take a crisp bite and
am on the ladder,
you holding the bowl,
we are peeling,
coring,
laying slices flat
for freezer bags,
clearing the dusty corners
of my mind.

2.
Keep some of the peel,
it thickens the sauce,
and yes, add a pinch more
cinnamon and some slivers
of ginger. It was always your
role to add sweetener.

Your hands,
never measuring, never scolding,
wrists bent in the curve of your paint brush,
knuckles rising and falling with your needle,
thumbs holding bows and wrapping paper,
fingers dipped in flour, shaping bread,
palms clasped together in prayer.

3.
Does your light shine brighter when I think of you?

4.
We are spreading thin crescents over
strudel dough that our fingers
pulled paper thin,
it splits in my budding hands,
and you patch it, a genesis of four hundred years,
collaboration of cultures, handwritten
recipes in dialects, generations that rebuilt lives
between wars, now a living family art.

You tell me of my great uncle
seven days on a boat from Europe to Canada,
the reason I was born in this country,
the reason we make this dish, to remember.

5.
Keep stirring. Grate some more nutmeg and add it.

Close your eyes and smell the fragrance till it rises
into the room, and you can step into the orchard again.

It is there that I find you every time.

6.
Why is it important to be remembered once we're gone?

7.
Drape a white cloth
over the table,
I tell you of forgotten apples
in abandoned orchards,
now labelled wild or heritage,
commemorated by research.

You once took off your jacket
knotted each sleeve,
stuffed them with wild apples,
and carried them over your shoulder.

During the war,
you once dropped your pack,
hoisted your weak grandmother
onto your shoulders
and carried her
to safety.

You planted memories with those seeds,
your story lives on,
your tree still grows.

8.
I see you in the quilted chair, hidden chocolates,
dangling threads, bare feet in the dew, papers tucked
in creased books, the mouths of snapdragons, unframed
photographs, your curly hair in the rain, ripe apples on
the cutting board.

9.
Wait now, before you ladle it into a bowl. You
have to let it cool first, flavours need time
to lock in.

I was impatient as a child, you once told me.
When I spoke, I wanted you to stop everything
and look into my eyes.

Now I'm waiting,
for your eyes,
again.

10.
Do you hear my thoughts when I write?

11.
You filled the freezer, lined the cellar with preserves.
All for later, next month. You always listened,
always gave - kind words, hugs, love - they were
part of every day.

12.
You are more than a memory,
you are the ageless hand of time,
the beating clock of my heart,
you are everywhere.

Red Tags

*For my childhood playground, Kirkpatrick's Forest,
before being cut down for a subdivision.*

One branch remains tagged,
a skeleton unburied,
its trunk dragged
between steel claws
along the forest floor.

I want to believe
this life binds us to something
with no red tags
no lingering questions;

that in one instant, we don't vanish,
taking our soul full of memories
and leaving behind sorrow.

I want to believe that next year
these trees will rise
in the root of a flower
sprouting in a garden

between rows of houses.

The Long Journey

It's a long journey
to find a place in this world.
Spring wildflowers know this,
burrowing their way
through darkness
till cool rains
seep into their skin.

They anchor themselves
deep in the earth, pushing
toward an unknown future,
summoned by a primal voice
deep inside
that whispers:

　　　Live.

　　　Grow.

Each flower makes
the difficult journey,
before the tree canopy
closes with thick foliage.

Trilliums cover the hillsides
their long pale fingers
rising from three broad leaves
like freshly fallen snow.

Mayapples unfurl
partially opened umbrellas
hiding a pale moon
under wings of green.

Although their life is brief,
each morning the moon petals
open their eyes,
lift their faces to the sun.

Standing among them,
my bare feet are drawn
through dry leaves
raking through
memory's dark cave

I'm summoned back

warm fingers
of light
lifting me off the ground.

The Forest of my Mind

Nothing is impossible
Everything can be overcome,
We must only wait
till our hearts are given wings.

I run into the rain,
turn outstretched arms
to the wind and fall
to my knees, silver
ribbons draping me,
till birds start singing,
flying above me
as if I were a tree.

            life here isn't weighted
            by the past
            it rises to each moment

I wipe the grass from my knees
clear the forest of my mind
This very act, my prayer to you.

Cover Me

...ragmen...
...of you, sl...
to my dai...
... There
... a date when ...
come to visi...
me when you ca... yo...
...st show up, r...
... in my m...
mid-sentence,
mid-chopping-onion,
mid-planting-a-garden,
...-talking-wit...
neighbours, mid-haircut,
mid-concert, mid-stargazin...
mid-brushing-teeth...
mid-driving-my-car,
mid-calling-the-plumbe...
mid-covering-your-tulips
from a frost.

You are always here.

...fragm...
...of yo...
... a part
...everything I do...
...et, wasn't...
...always t... an...
...ushering me in...
...world, you teaching
...guiding me, setting me
... to be independent an...
... my life: to be ch... oni...
ons, planting a garden, talking...
with neighbours, getting a
...rcut, going to a concert,
...gazing at stars, brushi...
my teeth, driving my car,
...alling a plumbe...
covering your tulips fro...
... a fros...

Lake Huron

They may have wondered
why I'm sitting in front
of the rolling waves,
wearing a down jacket,
bare toes wedged into the
cold sand.

Sorrow and loss is like that,
it doesn't see people walking by,
staring,
its too busy building a shrine for you
in the waves of my heart.

MOVING ON

Waiting

Your chair
sits where it always has —
waiting for you to fill it.

For the first time,
I sink into the soft cushion, rest
my hands on the wooden arms,
feel a compression of years
expanding in two directions —
your life and mine.

When I stand up,
I am older,
wiser,
I know what I want.

When I leave this earth,
I wish those I love to feel no pain,
I want to migrate into the darkness,
the light from my life
burning like a star
shining the way.

Ascension

The hawk swooped down
from the bright sky,
golden claws
snatching the fish
before it could
gasp or struggle.

Broad wings blocked
the crunch of bones
wild tearing of flesh.
When it lifted into the air,
the cinnamon red tail pointed
to the cartilage strewn
on flattened grass, one
clump of skin fluttering
into the arms of the wind.

Scales and gills ascend
within the hawk,
fuelling its flight.
Both are right now
swimming through the sun.

Into The Sun

The mourning dove
landed on a branch in front of me,
turned her gentle silver head
and looked into my eyes.

We were motionless for a long while,
time expanding as she stretched her fanned tail,
and I went to our fort in the woods,
our walks along the sandy beach,
our weekend cottage on the hill,
that stone castle in Germany.

Long after the dove looped into the sky,
I kept staring into her slate eyes,
I found you and lost you,
I fed you and buried you,
I sang to you and wept for you,
over and over again.

Every question I've asked,
every worry I've carried,
turned and fluttered,
flew into the bright sun.

The Future

Bold trills drift
from a river of trees,
a happy fountain of
song and laughter.

Sweet tunes float
smooth and angelic,
the kind you could
paint dreams from.

I know many bird calls
but not this one.

I prefer the mystery
under this ivory temple
of starlight

I don't want to know
everything, especially
not the future.

I don't want to lose
the absolute contentment
I feel right now
    looking into
    the bright face
    of the moon,

    complete and whole.

Sepia

I don't recognize
the face of this woman,
not even her name
scribbled on the
back: Sophia, Guelph.

Even if her last name
were written, I can't google her.
She would have no
website, no social
media. This is
my grandma's box
of photos. Sophia would
have been 125 this year.

My bookshelves
are filled with
albums from two
generations. Names

that carry no
memories to those
who have just
been born. It will be
the stuff
that gets boxed
for a thrift shop
or becomes landfill once
I'm gone. But for now
I stare at this

face I don't know,
a person that was
important
enough to be placed with
my grandma's pictures,
and wonder who she was,
what significance
her life had,
and if,
the young boy by her side,
is somewhere in
this world,
saying her name,
recalling memories
of a time well-lived.

Safe Shell

Each summer I wait for them
    to wake from their long sleep,
        emerge from the safe shell of moist earth,
            bioluminescence in our northern sky.

They burrow underground
    most of their lives
        waiting two years,
            for a hot summer night

to enter our world
    with their radiant flicker
        and live with a single
            purpose: to find a mate.

All evening long
    they blink and flash
        intricate patterns,
            looking for their own,

then wait through the day,
    in the safety of tall grasses,
        till the blue sky deepens
            to kindle the darkness again.

How sad to live so briefly,
    but at least they know
        their reason for being here.
            They live with intent.

We spend much of lives
    searching for ourselves,
        learning and stumbling,
            achieving and surrendering,

till we ultimately arrive
    at that final hour,
        to shed the shell
            of our own skin.

Fireflies don't even eat
    once they take first flight;
        two months is all they have,
            but look how they light up the night.

The Everyday

I waited,
on the sandy bottom
far from the deep reef
to feel them float over me,
fins enclosing my body
like wings.

I hesitated under their shadow,
mouths churning above my head.

I needed to slip into their world,
beyond the safety of mine,
to sit with bent knees in shallow waters
and sense the wildness in me —

       the fear
       the awe
       the vulnerability

       – and to know –
that nothing is supposed to be.
Nothing can be planned.
Nothing is greater than life itself.

I need to step over that edge.
Still.

Perseides Meteor
For Dad

Every year
far away from
city lights,
I watch them
set the sky on fire.

I saw them first
after your funeral,
climbing onto the rooftop
to see the tattooed night,
vast and infinite.

Was I looking for you?

They were a surprise,
in the middle of August.
We didn't know that
was their time
to burn down,
leaving a trail
dripping with light.

We didn't know
it was your time either,
early August.

What determines the hour?

Whatever force spins our
earth into debris trails of
broken asteroids, and colours
the folds of the evening,
I only need to think
of those falling stars when
the jaws of grief clamp down
on my heart.

You are a light in my life
                Always.
This night is ours.

Renewal

In spring, daffodil bulbs
lift the veil of damp earth,
opening their petals
in the hands of rain.

From a tree, a robin sings
pressing dry grasses and twigs
into a cup-shaped nest with
the wrist of her wing.

In the pond,
a chorus of spring peepers
rings like sleigh bells under
the curved neck of the moon.

Everything has returned
to its place,
but you.

If you ask me what I want,
it is days like this.
There is so much
beauty in our world,
let us forget the pain.

Your Turn

It's hard to move a walker
along a forest floor,
but it was your wish
to stand among
the golden lanterns of trees
to breathe in the moist air.

You knew time was closing in.
You said, *Now it's your turn,*
these are your years, not mine.

Like you,
I don't have one written list,
but I know my dreams,
what I hope for,
what I still want.

For you,
I will do everything
before I die.

Earthbound

i
When I arrived
earthbound from your womb,
your soothing voice anchored me
under the pull of skin,
weight of bones:

Everything started with you.

ii
The day your morphine drip arrived
everything happened so quickly,
we both knew it was time,
hope lay trapped
in the sun filtered window.

iii
You were the centre
of our family.

Everyone cared, listened,
came together,
for you.

iv
I am no longer a daughter.
A caregiver.

Those ended with you.

I've shed the skin of grief
the weight of sorrow,
waiting to be reborn.

A Snowflake Is Born

Right now,
high in the atmosphere,
a cold water droplet
encloses a strand of dust,
suspending it in ice.

The crystal tumbles
through darkness,
gathering moonbeams
and starlight, sprouting
six delicate arms
of lace, interlocking with
others, coasting in the arms
of the wind, until it lands
on my sleeve
soft and fragile, resting
under my breath, melting
without struggle, without fear.

Someday when death
enters the core of my body
bold and sharp, I want
to feel this serene,
knowing my precious life
was as bright as stars
full of wonder and laughter,
more giving than receiving.

Ebb and Flow

1.
I hear his exhalation
and breathe in.
An ebb and flow,
whale breath to mine.

He surfaces,
pushing the water aside
till it swells,
sliding effortlessly
back into the ocean,
slipping from one world
to another at whim.

It's a freedom I long for
— to travel without schedules,
chasing instinct,
not approvals.

2.
But I'm not here
to escape.
Sometimes I come to forget
for a brief period
my existence in this world.

3.
Like a periscope,
his fin rises six feet
out of the water,

his back emerges,
lifting the blue waves.
He swims toward us quickly,
sweeping the area for fish.

From this distance I see
his white patch, a permanent
smile circling his chin. Then
he takes another dive
and breaks through
farther away.

I strain my neck in his direction.
I wait, but he doesn't surface.

Come back.

I gather up the ocean.

Come back.

4.
I've always felt close to you
in the water, mother of my
womb, nurturer of my cells,
cultivator of my mind.

5.
Are we reborn each time we swim?

6.
I can only see his breath now,
mist rising,
circling the air.
I want to cast aside loss,
and disappointments,
dive into everything renewed.

You taught me how to swim,
through the eyes of the pond,
I flailed at first till
my limbs absorbed the primal
stirring, a knowing
older than the sea.

7.
There is wildness still
within each of us,
if we dare to look.
There is acceptance,
if we dare surrender the past.

The Mystery

Remember the cardboard
box, the noodles
worming into
the little beak,

    the flight?

Only a feather remained.

When I'm unwilling to leap,
I stand among the pines
and spread out my hand
to the young chickadee.

Claws wrapped around my finger, beak
picking a seed,
eyes stare,

      defenceless,

straight into mine
and I become
wild and human,
again, feather and skin.
Trusting the mystery.

INTERSECTION

Harvesting Seeds
For John

Autumn cradled her children
on barren earth, sent seed pods
spiraling into the raven sky,
but it has dropped snow today,
betraying her.

I don't know if my life is long, but
I believe in tomorrows, enough
so, that I scratch through the snow for
a handful of seeds. I dig into the cold
earth and scatter them.

But if this were my last hour,
I would spend it with you,
slow and full,
warm and bright,
knowing the love
we have sown and
nurtured, is infinite,
and will always be
our beacon.

Looking Deep

Early in the morning,
the turtle dove
puffs his translucent breast
and sends a low coo
from the roof corner,
in the same spot everyday,
content with his world.

If we could only be so lucky,
rather than wanting everything
easier, more
convenient.

Sometimes it's the challenges,
the hard work of looking deep
within, that teach us
how resilient we are,
how strong and capable
we stand.

I don't want anyone
to lighten my loss,
or make it gentler,
less complicated.
I want to feel the pain,
the uncertainty,
that gaping hole.

In time, I want to fill it myself
with birdsong,
walks in moonlight,
the mysteries of life.

Their World

Right now there's Marlowe,
and there will be others,
not yet born or named.
Pieces of me and you.

They giggle and coo,
then laugh and babble,
and someday will point
at your photo.

They will say your name,
learn your story,
and know you
as only a child can, with
the wisdom of intuition —
an innate sense of curiosity.

Someday when they're older,
and I am also gone,
    there will be a song they play,
    a word they speak,
    a gesture they utter,
    and it will be ours,
    a secret family code
    whispered in their bones.

Till then,
their world is ours.

For them I plant trees,
    fill bird feeders,
write poems,
    sing songs,
dance in the rain.

Still Breathing

I am an artifact
in this womb of the earth
gills blind to air
searching for you.

I leave myself behind,
surface between two worlds

this ocean of memory
breathing liquid
through my cells.

Finished

My fingers trace the ledge, decades
of shells picked along the beach,
rocks collected on walks.

My arms hold the weight
of your absence,
your unfinished projects,
half-written notes,
incomplete paintings,
clothes folded over your chair.

I don't have time to question anymore,
no open room for sorrow — there is so much
to be done.

I sing to you,
raise a chorus
and ring bells,
dip my fingers into the paint,
hands on paper

        hair

    water —

the sky is alive with our colours.

Intersection

1.
Before evening closes its door,
my fingers draw invisible lines
in the air
pinning three golden stars
against the bladed sky
across Orion's belt, five billion
years compressed
into a constellation name,
as we spiral through the Universe.

2.
Fingers draw your faces
in the air,
you are clouds climbing the freckled sky,
flowers closing their thin pages of silk,
trees swallowed by the moon.

Our three lives have a name,
our love is deep as this galaxy,
it expands with the hand of time.

3.
These are the two lines in my life:
your delicate fingers marking fabric,
every sketch since you were 17;
your strong hand measuring letters,
every blueprint and protractor arc.

My palm holds these pages,
leading me back home;
they are in my life daily,
our own bright stars.

4.
You couldn't have imagined,
when you sketched the sakko jacket,
that you would wear it across the ocean,
raising your children in a foreign language.

I see you swirling your skirt
on a hillside in Baden-Württemberg,
humming, a teen
heading for the train station,
dreaming wildly with daisies.

5.
And 27 kilometres away,
in Süßen station, you straighten
your tie and board a train,
full of determination
to build a better future.

You couldn't have planned it,
no matter how many
objects you drafted and calculated,
that you would travel overseas
write letters to your parents each week,
label every electrical drawing with new terms.

6.
Did it matter then,
that you would never
return to your homeland,
that you would live and die
on soil your ancestors never knew?

7.
Both of you had
a deep-seated wish
planted in your hearts,
feeling part of everything,
hopeful and alive.

On this page we are still together.

Déjà Vu

When I'm uncertain and unsure, this view holds me together,
a voice inside surfaces, breaks through, holds me together.

First a whisper, a distant hum, slides from the bowl of my life,
I spoon myself out, a new skin I step into, holds me together.

Should I be here? It's not for an answer, but a fervent prayer,
an unspoken promise. This secret taboo holds me together.

Can't take anyone here, can't share this, but I wait,
for a slow reckoning, old yet new holds me together.

You always come, if I wait. The scent, the shiver, the
familiar voice. This déjà vu holds me together.

Light shadows my eyes, turns me around. I hear:
your love so true holds me together.

The Forest of my Heart

In the forest of my heart
there is a path to you,
filled with feelings that wander
without destination.

Sometimes I find the path in silence,
without words or music,
guided by the secret
language of imagination.

Often my brothers and sisters
in the sky lead me.
They fly directly
into the wind's lashing tongue,
singing.

Years later even, I stumble,
when a simple reminder of you,
a song, a memory,
blurs my vision.

This is grief,
this heavy pain.
But then a melting away,
a kernel of hope.
This is returning

to the pond in the forest,
as it drinks the moon's reflection,
as the stars swirl in its bowl.

I surface
sifting, filling myself
with promise.

ACKNOWLEDGEMENTS

My heartfelt gratitude to you, the reader. For me, a pen and paper have always helped weave threads of loss and grief into a new understanding. This poetry collection touches upon the grief and loss I've experienced for various loved ones and it ends with hope and appreciation for the fragility and beauty of life. If you found yourself among these pages, I hope these poems brought a ray of peace to your loss.

I am very grateful to Lewis Slawsky and Alex Wall of Crowsnest Books for bringing this book into print. My deep appreciation to Jamie Arts for the cover design and interior layout which weaves together this entire collection. My heartfelt thanks to Theresa Albert for her energy and promotional talents. And thanks to Alan Chazaro, for his guidance on my final manuscript.

A very special thanks to Press 53 for selecting my poem "How We Live On" as the winner of their International Prime Number Magazine Poetry Award — this was a key moment for my poetry and the inspiration for many artistic collaborations based on this poem. My deep gratitude to filmmaker Kris von Kleist for seeing my poem "How We Live On" as a short film and for bringing that vision to the screen. My heartfelt thanks to David Eliakis for your friendship, your deep understanding of my poems, and for your amazing talent in composing and arranging music to my poetry. There are more artistic collaborations underway and I am grateful to all those creative individuals who were moved by my poetry and are interpreting it through their unique artistic expression.

My innermost thanks and appreciation to John for supporting me during the writing of this collection, with thoughtful insights and encouragement; and for being there during my years of grief — you are the one who sustains me and lifts me up. You, are the poetry in my life.

In my early years, it was my parents that offered comfort, and it is their very departure from this planet that inspired much of this poetry. Thanks Mom and Dad, for always supporting my creative endeavours. Thanks also to my family who shared that journey of grief and loss.

I want to also thank Jaime Lee Mann and Pete Conrad for their valued readings, keen insight, and ongoing support while I was pulling this collection together. A heartfelt thanks to my sister Renate for encouraging me when I was a very young poet. And deep gratitude to my dear friend Heather for her daily encouragement and support.

Finally, a thanks to all those who have been a part of my growth as a writer: Carol Jankowski, Jim Reid, Nancy Rotozinski, Joyce Eichholz and Edith Janke.

The world is a better place with people who appreciate that arts and support those creating it. Variations of these poems have been recited and performed at events and funerals, in forests and canoes, at bedsides and dinner tables. I gratefully acknowledge the following publications, in which poems from this book have previously appeared, sometimes in slightly different form:

Prime Number Magazine: How We Live On
*winner of the International Prime Number Magazine Poetry Award

Pasque Petal: Into The Sun, Ascension, Safe Shell

Tiny Seed Journal: Snow and Sky

Rise Up Anthology: The Forest of my Mind, Finished

Minerva Rising: Intersection

Plant People, An Anthology of Environmental Artists: The Long Journey

Snapdragon: A Journal of Art & Healing: Fill This Room

Undercurrents: The Everyday, Still Breathing

Footsteps Along The Grand: Red Tags, The Mystery

As I started this book, I would like to leave the last thought for my mom, a talented poet herself, and the most precious heart I have ever known. You are forever with me, mom.

Heidi Sander

ABOUT THE AUTHOR

Writing and storytelling are at the heart of everything Heidi Sander touches. She is a bestselling author, international award-winning poet, and Pushcart Prize nominee whose poems have been published in literary journals, recited at everything from conferences to funerals and in forests as well as canoes. From film to music, artists have collaborated with her to create works based on her poems. She also has extensive experience in the publishing world as the founder of Blue Moon Publishers, the Stratford Writers Festival, and DigiWriting book marketing agency. She has developed an online program, *Pathways to Poetry*, to help poets find their voice, publish their writing, and promote their work: bit.ly/PathwaysToPoetry

heidisander.com

Facebook: @heidisanderwriter

Instagram: @heidisanderwriter

ALPHA LISTING